T0349054

Praise fo
6 Lineage Poems

"Fernando Trujillo's *6 Lineage Poems* is an exquisite collection that considers literary, cultural, and familial inheritance. A welcome queer response to Stevens, the sequence '13 Ways of Nepantla' combines lines from Neruda and Whitman—those great poets of the people—to explore the Chicano and Latino concept of liminality (all while maintaining an elegant structural design). From the opening poem's cairn that collapses in a shallow lake of the mind to the final poem's pebble that makes a ripple in the lake of a public garden, this balanced collection deserves to be read and reread slowly, rapturously. Reminding us of the danger and vulnerability that poetry demands, Trujillo writes, 'The only place I knew to go was the heart / of your soul dark as the darkest iron. How I wanted / your gold—you who pulled a gun on me while / I did nothing but lean into the barrel.'"

—CAROLYN HEMBREE, contest judge and author of *For Today*

"Fernando Trujillo's sensuous, romantic poems sing 'in tears, / in rapture, in love, in ruins.' Under the sign of Lorca, they consummately balance baroque excess and total intimacy, exploring the delights and agonies of relationships, ancestries, and the erasures of shame—'a man's most important work,' as one poem describes it. The poet of *6 Lineage Poems*, as forthright as he is erudite, reaches back into the traditions of literature—from a range of times, places, and languages—in order to make something fresh, vigorous, perfect."

—RICHIE HOFMANN, author of *A Hundred Lovers*

"Through reprisals and erasures, Fernando Trujillo's *6 Lineage Poems* accounts for the feverish motions and fiery undersides of want, tuning poetic forebearers to conjure a many-tongued América that is more choral incantation than solitary verse. Employing both ekphrasis and epistolary, Trujillo begs the distinctions between jealousy and envy, shame and desire, romance and passion, and the question of an addressee: wayward, distanced, absent, always. Through misrecognition and the embrace of obscurity, Trujillo's speakers transform any sense of a stable subject into the music of a new lyric: 'Make of me a song.'"

—CHRIS CAMPANIONI, author of *VHS* and *North by North/west*

"There is a massive charge pulsing through the lines of Fernando Trujillo's poems. His words are electric, brimming with life and longing. In *6 Lineage Poems*, Trujillo weaves sequences that eloquently navigate the intersections of desire and shame, landscape and language into a stunning web of music and breathtaking imagery: 'That curve / where the small / of his back ended, / copper-forged anvil in moonlight...' This marks the advent of a powerful voice in American poetry."

—ALDO AMPARÁN, author of *Brother Sleep*

"Reading Trujillo's chapbook feels like slipping into a rapturous spring dream on a winter night, where the reader is invited to enter the nepantla—a space between worlds—immersed in the layered dimensions of cultures, rich literary traditions, languages, and the erotic tension between self and other. Hold your breath; in Trujillo's poems, each line pulses with duende."

—SHANGYANG FANG, author of *Burying the Mountain*

"*6 Lineage Poems* begins in quiet love and unfurls into expansive paeans to memory and sensation. Taking cues from Lorca, Stevens, and Tang dynasty poets, Trujillo journeys from 'el instante of being / in two lands' in El Paso to a sonnet sequence about 'the heavenly hellish cage' of romance. Read Trujillo's tender, artful poems to savor the everyday, to disentangle desire, and to reinvigorate the self. 'My blessings are a mountain, so I stand,' he writes, and these poems are blessings, too."

—REUBEN GELLEY NEWMAN, author of *Feedback Harmonies*

"En el instante of being / in two lands / tocayo / was it loss you felt?' writes Trujillo, whose poems are at once lyric invocations and stirring declarations, all of them asking us to reckon with the tension of eros in corporeal and geographic borderlands. *6 Lineage Poems* tends the multiplicity of inheritance with intensity and attention while allowing the nuances of grief to manifest as literal erasure. These are finely crafted poems indeed, and only build anticipation for the stunning debut to come."

—MEG DAY, author of *Last Psalm at Sea Level*

6 Lineage Poems

6 Lineage Poems

Fernando Trujillo

Winner of The 2024 Robert Phillips Chapbook Prize
Selected by Carolyn Hembree

TRP: THE UNIVERSITY PRESS OF SHSU
HUNTSVILLE, TEXAS 77341

Copyright © 2025 Fernando Trujillo
All Rights Reserved

Library of Congress Cataloging-in-Publication Data
Names: Trujillo, Fernando, 1990- author.
Title: 6 lineage poems / Fernando Trujillo.
Other titles: Six lineage poems
Description: First edition. | Huntsville, Texas : TRP, The University Press
  of SHSU, 2025.
Identifiers: LCCN 2024041872 (print) | LCCN 2024041873 (ebook) | ISBN
  9781680034127 (trade paperback) | ISBN 9781680034134 (ebook)
Subjects: LCGFT: Poetry.
Classification: LCC PS3620.R8565 A614 2025 (print) | LCC PS3620.R8565
  (ebook) | DDC 811/.6--dc23/eng/20240911
LC record available at https://lccn.loc.gov/2024041872
LC ebook record available at https://lccn.loc.gov/2024041873

FIRST EDITION

Cover art photo was taken by the poet's father in the family backyard
Cover design by Cody Gates, Happenstance Type-O-Rama
Interior design by Maureen Forys, Happenstance Type-O-Rama

Printed and bound in the United States of America
First Edition Copyright: 2025

TRP: The University Press of SHSU
Huntsville, Texas 77341
texasreviewpress.org

Winner of the 2024 Robert Phillips Chapbook Prize

Selected by Carolyn Hembree

Established in 2001, The Robert Phillips Poetry Chapbook Prize highlights one book per year that excels in the chapbook format.

Previous Winners:

Christine Kitano, *Dumb Luck & other poems*

J. L. Conrad, *Recovery*

Marisa Tirado, *Selena Didn't Know Spanish Either*

Elizabeth Murawski, *Still Life with Timex*

Thomas Nguyen, *Permutations of a Self*

Gregory Byrd, *The Name for the God Who Speaks*

Evana Bodiker, *Ephemera*

Mark Schneider, *How Many Faces Do You Have?*

Loueva Smith, *Consequences of a Moonless Night*

J. Scott Brownlee, *Ascension*

Harold Whit Williams, *Backmasking*

David Lanier, *Lost and Found*

John Popielaski, *Isn't It Romantic?*

Ingrid Browning Moody, *Learning About Fire*

David Havird, *Penelope's Design*

Rebecca Foust, *Mom's Canoe*

Rebecca Foust, *Dark Card*

Lisa Hammond, *Moving House*

Taylor Graham, *The Downstairs Dance Floor*

Kevin Meaux, *Myths of Electricity*

Ann Killough, *Sinners in the Hands: Selections from the Catalog*

Nancy Naomi Carlson, *Complications of the Heart*

William Notter, *More Space Than Anyone Can Stand*

Contents

Water, is taught by thirst.

—EMILY DICKINSON, no. 135

Quiet Night Thought

Moon
in the lake
vast
in wet skies
I wade in
to reach you,
smooth stones
underfoot—
cold rises from calf
to chest
but still
you're too
far,
blancor almidonado
bright.

A cairn in shallow waters
collapses—

Were I braver,
I'd chase you
into
the
depths.

13 Ways of Nepantla

I was of three minds,
Like a tree
In which there are three blackbirds.
—WALLACE STEVENS

[1]
Throats thick with tobacco and mezcal.
Reverberations of violence,
ecstasies and transformations.
Sizzle of nopales on the grill.

[2]
Roaming downtown EP after the OP,
full of drink and the taste of men—
noche de ronda, frightening awake
a black dove before dawn.

[3]
En el instante of being
in two lands
tocayo
was it loss you felt?
Does a body crossing
mark across the body?

[Chorus]
América America,

brazos de agua
swinging from the boughs—
del aire al aire the
varied carols I hear—

[4]
Tia abuela Ñeca rolls out rising
balls of dough in Arizona,
tortillas off the comal,
dozens of fresh empanadas laid
out for the sticky fingers of a child
who pledges allegiance to a flag
each day in school.

[5]
Along the railroad track
one foot in front of
the other on the rusted out
rail beneath Mt Cristo Rey,
pennies laid out, waiting
for the thrill of a roiling
tingle as the train rushes by,
flattening what
was worth so little
to him.

[6]
A penny saved
is a penny less of frijoles
for dinner,

Tencha states,
slaving over a stovetop,
getting a college degree.

[7]
Young flesh
Friday night in Juárez,
delicious cumbia raíz
off her hips,
the beat shakes—
Lupe cutting
up the dance floor.

[Chorus]
América America,
brazos de agua
swinging from the boughs—
del aire al aire the
varied carols I hear—

[8]
Sauce de cristal-formed timestone in the sun
-old capital, son of Aztec and colonizer
holding out a hand to touch its edge. Chingado nieto
de La Malinche reaching up to grasp for the meaning
of blood hating blood in one vein.

[9]
I don't like spics, says the brown boy
sitting at an overlook on Transmountain,
I like that you look white;
or,

I don't know why they sent *her,*
the boss says,
I've already met my quota.

[10]
On a cliffside bus,
Veinte poemas in his lap,
condor lazing among the
heights above Iruya.

[Chorus]
América America,
brazos de agua
swinging from the boughs—
del aire al aire the
varied carols I hear—

[11]
A home made in
the pass between the mountains.

[12]
A 3 coo-weaved-counterpoint
at odds and in harmony,
refusing to be caged.

[13]
She sings
sing to me, cántame.
But I tell myself it really means
sing me to me.
Make of me a song.

[Chorus]
América America,
brazos de agua
swinging from the boughs—
del aire al aire the
varied carols I hear—

Child With Closed Eyes

after Federico García Lorca

That curve
where the small
of his back ended,
copper-forged anvil
in moonlight, us
in his truck bed, wet
from the drizzle
of sweat and rain,
him and every other him,
them and every other them—
that, too, was you—
you who lingered
nights and days among
the sounds of gritos
and guitars in the desert,
where we wailed,
lo más juntos, one
with a city and
river and mountain—
in tears, in rapture,
in love and in ruins
o how we sang,
danced, threw and
thrashed ourselves.
You seemed
a beauty of stone—
much like those
switchbacks above Zion.
But it was not so,
child with closed eyes.

An Approach and Nothing More
after Megan Fernandes

1.
Day cascades into a fiery sunset,
us in bed, sweat cooling on our skin.

You wrote me a sestina and called it
love. But you ignore me in public, even

if now you're relentless in sweet words as you
fuck me, gently tickling my head after.

Feverish motion is overtaken by a stillness
that blurs at the edges—your nearness

overwhelms—even in our exhaustion your
skin on mine electrifies. We listen to Nina sing

Black is the Color of My True Love's Hair.

A sprinkling of rain splatters the window. Now
the little spoon, your thick hair fills my hands.

I know you'll forget this when you leave.

Day cascades into

       relentless   sweet words
fuck me

                  stillness

overwhelms
       . We listen to

    the Color of

sprinkling   rain splatters   . Now
           my hands

   forget   .

2.

You, my two-day lover cycling across the continent,
told me to visit the Mapplethorpe exhibit, and I wonder,
why is the muscle-dom holding the chain
not kissing his boy? Maybe I only think that because,

as I look at the mounted photo, I feel
your hungry mouth on my neck. I touch myself,
there. I think I came here looking for your blue shirt and
dust-caked biker shorts, but what I've found instead

is shame, a man's most important work tucked
into a cordoned-off, out-of-the-way corner, segregated
from the flowers and Patti Smith. Which just reminds me
of you telling me on the second day about your

fiancée. Shame. Now I sit under a waxing crescent,
caring so little about you my bones shake.

          two-day
            visit
                    holding the
      kissing   boy Maybe I

      look
        hungry   . I touch
        I think

    shame, a man's most important work

                        . Which just reminds me
  of   your

  fiancée. Shame. Now I sit
              about   my bones   .

3.

What was that kiss if not a wish in black with
you who kept my cheeks stained. You never
said goodbye to me yet you are gone as
your lungs filled with smoke, coughing into me

a ready-made despair. Again and again I ran
nowhere but into your cruel embrace that called
like the tolling bell. How I surrendered.
There was no sweetness in you; was there ever—

The only place I knew to go was the heart
of your soul dark as the darkest iron. How I wanted
your gold—you who pulled a gun on me while
I did nothing but lean in into the barrel.

The proof of me lived in your promise,
and I was naught but the biggest of fools.

What   with
                    cheeks stained

     lungs   coughing

                                    again I ran

                         .   surrendered.

                                        heart
                              iron
          gold—you

     proof of me,
       I   naught but   of   .

4.

A season spent among the birds, flitting
from one branch to another, paired in embrace.

But it's winter now, and the birds are away. *Cry
Me a River* Barbra sings out in black and white.

I realize I have more jealousy in me than I'm willing
to admit. Or is it envy? I didn't mind the clients,

but seeing you hold him hurt more than I'd have rather
borne. It felt like a question of when, not if, I'd lose you.

Maybe I'm not as open-minded as I give myself
credit for. How many times have I left men

for whom I've cared, trying to beat them to the punch?
I walk out of your luxury condo, heavenly hellish cage,

and book a flight home. *Cry Me a River* Barbra sings out
in black and white; I wonder to whom she's singing

                    to   embrace

    winter   ,   *Cry*

                                            .

I realize   I'm willing
        .   envy didn't

                    hurt more than
                                            you.

Maybe   I give myself
                            men

        I've cared   to   punch
    out,   heavenly hellish cage,

                    home.   *a river*   sings
            ;

                            she's singing.

5.

Tonight you dance on other shores
with other people while I remain at a distance
that can only be measured in leagues, you so far
out of mine it can only be measured in time: millennia,

eons. Your evening's story unfolds as you sway
beer in hand sweat down your tank top singing
a song I cannot hear, face flushed in a blazing heat
of joy radiating kindness as you smile and speak and be—

I would feel like a thief in your arms, so I supplicate
to the sands of the Chihuahuan which are vast because
only their vastness deserves your depths.

Your eyes curve up questioningly—
in your sigh I find an answer to my prayer;
it is answered with a crush, a scent that follows.

people   remain

                far
         in time

.

         you sway

      like a thief   I supplicate

only

  eyes
    sigh   my prayer
              follows.

6.
Flowing grain like granite soft
brown on white hyacinth melanin
in waves swirling across your torso;
I follow its outline with my tongue. Eyes

flutter nearing sleep, lips on your V—you
pull me up to your face, wrapping your arms
around my body, nuzzling your head
into the crook of my neck.

Windows open, it's been a warm winter,
which is to say the weather has been clean,
smooth; the breeze's coolness rubs our rough
edges; you pull the ermine blanket across us.

Tomorrow piques at the mind like always,
the prospect of a season, or of a life.

soft

waves
        outline   my tongue

          , lips
              wrapping your
     body
into   my neck

   ,

                   clean
     breeze[] coolness

           .

       the mind
    a season,   a life.

7.

God knows my motions—I cannot deceive
Them, though I try. Do I love, or

do I despair—I ask myself this as you pant near-
breathless this first night of passion between us,

or is it, too, the last? I gave myself to you because
you are beautiful (I value beauty more
than I should), and you were kind, and I am
weak. When I was young, I prayed to God,

asked Them for Ecstasy. Perhaps They responded
too liberally. Stroke me there again, kiss me,
again; I will not die in the knowledge of your ephemeral
touch. Too dear you are for my wallet—too dear am I for

your heart. The world about us is in shambles, but tonight
I am electric, and you are the architecture of my desire.

you are beautiful

,   I am

weak.

    I will   die

                             in shambles, but

    electric   .

8.
Horizon shades of dried blood bookstore
closing home calling though I do not want to
go me all that awaits in spades black and sharp.
I've been too much even for myself lately.
Is oblivion erasure or unmitigated immensity,
I ask no one in particular, seated on a curb
wondering what makes the colors of the sky
—unable to make myself rise.

Every lover has passed, in their own way.
Am I allowed to say, "I don't want to be alone?"
Maybe I always will be; after all, I can be
a lot to handle, here there everywhere
manic depressive that I am. But what of it.
My blessings are a mountain, so I stand.

Yet—Hear—

When you left, outside my window,
was it in bloom—that winter plum?
—WANG WEI

1.

Migration north to south, east to west: a devotion of movement like of a swallow to América from Texas in autumn.

Spinning along this black asphalt expanse, in the road fate's crush splits into a thousand-petaled wildflower.

2.

Scythe at harvest, slashing. Sweat on the brow. Gun held and shot, at pigeons clay and flesh.

Bird eaten. Earth tasted.

Happiness is a feeling.

Touching the wall, coarseness comes through.

3.

The city in a flowing stream of sound; a lakeside where the moon was loudest. I do not know which I prefer.

From the train tracks curving along the base of the mountain, a rhythm of steel on steel. Fountain gurgle—dog bark—the shortening whip of an ambulance pulling away.

Perhaps the city is quieter than I think, and the lakeside was filled with its own music. "Perhaps" offers silken comfort and velvet danger.

If memory serves me right, it never does.

Forgetting: a thing I do too easily.

4.

Howl of heat dripping sweat, jalapeños ripe

Mother's garden is green. The soil is rich, fingernails caked.

Unmoored by the sting of the sun and the lines of my hand and the moisture of my breath, I close my eyes.

5.
Grey-bottomed morning clouds hug mountain peaks, their own peaks golden with light.

A school bus picks up children, people go to work. The cold bundles me in layers.

6.
In the whistling wind a flock lands on power lines.

Park empty, I lie on the tennis court.

The wind is cool, sun hot. All this warmth beneath me, oceanic sky above.

Magnolias flutter, bird shit mingling in my beard.

7.
Distant whir of the interstate—one bird's coo, another's chirp.

Brush of oleander branches that I can't see, seated here beneath the window.

As if from nowhere: a train's horn.

After, Considering

Sliver of your wrist between the stacks, slender. You push up your glasses as I try so hard to pull your eyes into mine from across the room; then there they are; are you blushing?

My God.

A Chopin scherzo, my favorite, comes on over the speakers as you smile at something said. It is enough—the afternoon billows out from itself.

In the open air, the winter warmth of Phoenix as I walk to the Japanese Friendship Garden.

On my bench, book closed beside me, I watch two boys lean one into the other, gravel underfoot of passerby. So many couples, lovely in private conversations, laughter. The blue-green lake calms, waterfall dimming the sounds of the garden's audience. Water plops—

I
am
small—
contain
nothing—
little
pebble
splash
ripples.

c/s

Notes

1. The collection's epigraph comes from poem no. 135 by Emily Dickinson.

2. "Quiet Night Thought," which first appeared with *Passages North*, is titled after a Li Bai poem of the same name. The phrase "blancor almidonado" is from Federico García Lorca's "Romance de la luna, luna."

3. "13 Ways of Nepantla" first appeared with *Michigan Quarterly Review* (Laurence Goldstein Prize in Poetry). It was additionally featured on *Poetry Daily*. The epigraph is from Wallace Stevens' "Thirteen Ways of Looking at a Blackbird," which also inspired the title and structure. "...del aire al aire" is from Pablo Neruda's "Alturas de Macchu Picchu" and "...the / varied carols I hear" is from Walt Whitman's "I Hear America Singing." The phrase "Sauce de cristal" is from Octavio Paz's "Piedra de sol."

4. "Child With Closed Eyes'" title is inspired by, and the poem is after, Federico García Lorca's "Romance de la luna, luna."

5. "An Approach and Nothing More" is titled after a phrase from C. P. Cavafy's "Half an Hour" as translated by Edmund Keely and Philip Sherrard. The poem sequence itself is after a sequence from Megan Fernandes's *I Do Everything I'm Told*. "Black is the Color of My True Love's Hair" is in reference to the song as sung by both Nina Simone and Emil Latimer. "Cry Me a River" is in reference to the version sung by Barbra Streisand.

6. "Yet—Hear—"'s title comes from Wang Wei's "Deer Park" as translated by Gary Snyder. The epigraph comes from "Untitled," by Wang Wei, translated by David Hinton, from *THE SELECTED POEMS OF WANG WEI*, copyright © 2006 by David Hinton. Reprinted by permission of New Directions Publishing Corp.

Acknowledgments

This collection would not have been possible without the support of my family, in particular that of my loving parents with their seemingly endless patience. I'd also like to acknowledge the mentorship of Richie Hofmann, who has been gracious with his time and consideration. Additionally, I'd like to express gratitude for Bill Clark at my local indie bookshop in El Chuco (Literarity), Miguel Ángel García, Jr. for reading my work and providing critical feedback/encouragement, and also for Aldo Amparán and and jj peña for their support.

I'd also like to extend my gratitude to Carolyn Hembree for seeing something in my work, and to J. Bruce Fuller, Charlie Tobin, and everyone at TRP for their care and attention in helping bring this project into the world.